TRUE
Worship

Colin Urquhart

Kingdom Faith Resources Ltd.
Roffey Place, Old Crawley Road,
HORSHAM West Sussex, RH12 4RU
Tel: 01293 851543 Fax: 01293 854610
E-mail: resources@kingdomfaith.com
www.kingdomfaith.com

First published in Great Britain in March 2003 by Kingdom Faith

Kingdom Faith Trust is a registered charity (no.278746)

ISBN 1-900409-41-0

Acknowledgements

I praise God for opening the way for us to draw near to Him in worship, to be able to meet with Him in His holiness and experience His glory. I pray that this short book will open your eyes to what is possible for you, if you allow the Holy Spirit to lead you in worship.

I am thankful to the Lord for all at Kingdom Faith who have shared together in the wonderful move of God that has taken place for several years, and in which the worship has played such a significant part. My thanks also to Mary, David and Cliss for all they have done in the presentation of this book.

As always, to God belongs all the glory!

Colin Urquhart

CONTENTS

1

WHAT IS WORSHIP?

There are three distinct ways in which we can speak of worship. First, there is the overall sense in which every area of our lives is to be lived in "worship" of God, meaning that we want to glorify Him in all we do, to live for Him rather than for ourselves. Paul says:

> *Therefore, I urge you, brothers, in view of God's mercy,*
> *to offer your bodies as living sacrifices, holy and pleasing to God –*
> *this is your spiritual act of worship.*
> *(Romans 12: 1)*

The word translated "worship" here means to worship by serving. If we offer God our bodies, then we offer Him our hearts, souls, every aspect of our being contained within the body. Obviously if we have truly given the Lord our hearts, then we have also offered Him our bodies, for a heart without a body cannot love, serve, bless, give. The body expresses what is contained in the heart.

It would make little sense to worship God with our mouths, if the lives we lived were a contradiction to the things we verbalised to Him. This would be a form of hypocrisy, a subject the Lord addresses in scripture to impress upon His people how offensive such worship is to Him. *"These people honour me with their lips, but their hearts are far from me,"* He says. Such worship is in vain!

The truth is that when He died for you on the cross, Jesus purchased you for God with His own blood. Therefore you are to *"honour God with your body." (1 Corinthians 6: 20)* Your body is now a temple of the Holy Spirit. He lives in you to express the life of Jesus in you and to cause His life to flow from you to others that you might be a blessing to them.

To co-operate with the Lord is to worship Him with your body and your life! In this series of books, several titles contain teaching about what it means to live as disciples, to glorify God with our hearts and bodies. So we are not going to speak of this aspect of "worship" in this book, except to say that all true worship will be set within the context of a life that is lived to please God.

Secondly, people think of worship as addressing the Lord in thanksgiving, praise and prayer, whether personally, independent of others, or corporately in a church service. Such "worship" may take several different forms and can involve a number of different activities.

All Christians have some experience of "worship," in this understanding of the word, whether in a formal, liturgical church service, or a more informal meeting where the "worship" will be more spontaneous.

There are also many differences as to participation in such "worship." Liturgical forms may be led by a priest or minister, with the congregation's part reduced to the singing of a few hymns or choruses, plus the making of certain liturgical responses. In other church meetings, the gifts of the Spirit may operate more freely, and participation of the congregation in the exercise of these gifts may be encouraged.

Let the word of Christ dwell in you richly as you teach and admonish one another with all wisdom, and as you sing psalms, hymns and spiritual songs with gratitude in your hearts to God. (Colossians 3: 16)

The apostle, Paul, says something similar when writing to the Ephesians:

Speak to one another with psalms, hymns and spiritual songs. Sing and make music in your heart to the Lord, always giving thanks to God the Father for everything, in the name of our Lord Jesus Christ. (Ephesians 5: 19-20)

Paul speaks of addressing our praise to the Lord and also singing or speaking to one another, encouraging each other with the truth of who God is and what He has done for us. Clearly, from what he says, Paul sees such "worship" as an expression of what is happening continuously in our lives. As believers we are to *"Be joyful always; pray continually; give thanks in all circumstances, for this is God's will for you in Christ Jesus." (1 Thessalonians 5: 16-18)*

So when meeting together, Christians are to encourage one another by thanking, praising God and praying to Him, as they would when alone. In this way they are helping to build up the corporate life of the Body of Christ.

Now clearly it is good to do all these things. As one who has travelled in ministry to many parts of the world, I can testify to the immense range of the styles of such "worship"! Some are certainly more anointed than others. Some seem to touch God in real and personal ways, especially at certain times. However, this seems to depend more on the spiritual state of those worshipping or on the way someone is leading the meeting. There is very rarely the expectation that because they are worshipping, the people will certainly be able to draw near to the throne of God, have personal encounter with Him and experience His glory.

Yet this is what God intends. Although we can rightly call such forms as "worship" in a general sense, they fall some way short of what God intends and of what the scriptures describes as "worship" in a more particular way.

Let me repeat, it is essential that Christians obey these scriptures: That they pray on their own as Jesus instructs, and together as the Body of Christ in their local congregations. It is right to sing songs and hymns to one another to encourage one another, and to the Lord in thanksgiving for what He has done. Yet anybody familiar with such "worship" knows only too well that it is possible to do these things, without our hearts necessarily being engaged with God, without meeting with Him personally in His glory, and without His Spirit impacting us in life-dwelling ways.

Third: the most common word for "worship" in both the Old and New Testaments means to "bow" or "stoop down" before the One being worshipped. God has given us insight into the worship in heaven where those around His throne worship like this.

Jesus has made it possible to approach the very throne of grace, to join with the heavenly host in meeting with the Lord in His majestic holiness and glory. This does not need to be an occasional experience when a time of worship seems particularly anointed, but can be our experience whenever we choose to worship the Lord in spirit and truth, as Jesus commands us.

Even many pentecostal and charismatic believers are not familiar with such worship. For many worship is regarded as an activity that precedes the preaching of the Word, or as a time to rejoice and have an enjoyable time. They do not expect to have a personal encounter with the Holy One, or to be able to know His glory.

Such things are not only possible, but the Lord's instruction for us. In this book we are going to concentrate in particular on this third understanding of the word "worship," and we will learn from the scriptures how it is possible for any born again believer to meet with God in this way.

These three meanings of "worship" can be said to describe the three main areas of the temple. The outer court contained the altar of sacrifice. Here we live daily that our bodies may be a living sacrifice, *"holy and acceptable to the Lord."*

The middle court, is the Holy Place, where the priests carried the offerings. We can liken this to the songs and hymns that one sings to the Lord, the "worship" that at times causes us to be aware of the Lord's Presence, but lacking what is possible in the inner court.

This is the Holy of holies, the dwelling place of God among His people. Under the old covenant only the High Priest was allowed to enter the Holy of holies and then only once a year, on the Day of Atonement to pray for the forgiveness of his sins and those of the whole nation.

On the cross, Jesus opened up the way into the heavenly sanctuary, the new Holy of holies, for every believer. Now we can all enter His Holy Presence, encounter Him in His glory while still on earth. We do not have to be content with the Holy Place. God wants us in the Holy of Holies.

There His presence is such that, like the heavenly beings, we "bow" before, we "stoop down," we are on our faces before His awesome glory. This is the worship that is truly pleasing to the Lord, for Jesus tells us to pray that His will is to be done on earth as it is in heaven. If this is how heaven is able to worship, this is how we on earth are able to worship "in spirit and in truth."

2

IN SPIRIT AND TRUTH

"Never have I experienced such a sense of the Presence of God in worship." This is typical of the statements made by well-travelled international speakers, who have spoken at our conferences and services at Kingdom Faith, people who have experienced worship in many forms and styles.

Is it really possible to have a personal encounter with God whenever we worship Him? Or is this something that can only happen infrequently when God chooses to move in a particular way? Can we really meet with Him in His holiness and glory whenever we choose to do so?

Perhaps not all that people call "worship" is true worship of the kind God desires! Jesus said:

> *Yet a time is coming and has now come when the true*
> *worshippers will worship the Father in spirit and truth, for they*
> *are the kind of worshippers the Father seeks. (John 4: 23)*

God the Father seeks worshippers, people with hearts of worship, those whose nature is to worship Him. **Jesus does not see worship**

JESUS DOES NOT SEE WORSHIP AS AN ACTIVITY, BUT AS THE HEART EXPRESSION OF THOSE WHO KNOW AND LOVE HIM.

as an activity, but as the heart expression of those who know and love Him. It is not the form of the worship that concerns Him, but the heart condition of the worshippers.

The worshippers the Father desires are those who worship "in spirit and in truth." He is not interested in a performance. Rather He wants the human spirits of the worshippers to be engaged with His Spirit, allowing the worshipper to be drawn into the unity with Him that He desires.

God is spirit, and his worshippers must worship in spirit and in truth. (John 4: 24)

This is not an option, but a necessity. This is the way Christians *must* worship: in spirit and in truth!

First, let us consider what the word "worship" means. This is literally to give worth to someone who is the object of your devotion. To worship God is to express to Him what He is worth!

Immediately we are confronted with an impossibility, for it is not possible to express adequately in words God's true worth! However, we can look to the Bible, for there are many passages of worship in the scriptures. To learn what it means to worship in spirit and in truth will throw us onto dependence on the revelation that scripture gives us of the worship in heaven. For all that takes place there is in "spirit and truth."

When teaching how we are to pray, Jesus makes it clear that God wants His Kingdom and His will to be expressed on earth as it is in heaven. This means He wants "heavenly" worship here on earth! Is such worship possible? Most certainly. And God has given us His Spirit to make such worship possible for those who believe in Him.

Worship is literally, to "bow" or "stoop down" as an act of submission and reverence towards the one being worshipped. This is to be the willing response of the one worshipping: it is not something forced on him or her. It is to pay homage freely to the one being worshipped.

Jesus is saying that true worshippers will pay homage to God, will bow before Him in reverent submission. They must do this from their hearts, not merely as an outward gesture; with absolute sincerity and integrity in a way pleasing to the Lord.

In the Old Testament, the Book of Psalms contains many ascriptions of worship that express this truth:

> *Exalt the LORD our God and worship at his footstool;*
> *he is holy. (Psalm 99: 5)*

In only a few words, the Psalmist is compressing several important truths about worship. The worshipper wants to "exalt the Lord," to lift Him up, to magnify Him, to focus on His greatness. By contrast, the worshipper is paying homage to Him by bowing at His feet, in loving and reverent submission to His greatness.

God is holy by nature; He is whole, complete, perfect in Himself. The worshipper is only too aware of his or her own unworthiness before such an awesome God. And yet the wonderful truth is that God wants us to draw near to Him for He longs to reveal Himself in His glory and holiness to His people. Because of all that Jesus had done for us on the cross, cleansing us of our sin and unworthiness, it is possible for us to approach His throne without fear of judgment and to meet with Him in His glory and majesty. However, even though we are made clean by His blood, and are given access right to the throne of God's grace we are still as nothing before Him.

WE WORSHIP HIM AS HE NOW IS, THE LORD OF GLORY, THE MOST HIGH, THE HOLY ONE

John, the apostle, had a relationship with Jesus, closer than the other disciples and certainly understood Him better. At the Last Supper, he lay with His head on the breast of Jesus. Yet this same John, who was able to enjoy such intimacy with Jesus in His humanity, responded very differently years later when He met with Him in His glory!

When I saw him, I fell at his feet as though dead.
Then he placed his right hand on me and said: "Do not be afraid.
I am the First and the Last." (Revelation 1: 17)

We do not worship Jesus as He was in the days of His humanity. **We worship Him as He now is, the Lord of Glory, the Most High, the Holy One,** *"majestic in holiness, awesome in glory."* *(Exodus 15: 11)*

The root of the Greek word means to kiss. To worship is to kiss the feet of Jesus; to worship and adore Him out of a heart of love. It will be obvious, therefore, that worship is not simply the singing of hymns or songs to God. It is to involve the drawing near to Him, a humbling of ourselves before Him in reverence. It involves a personal encounter with God, a meeting with Him!

However, it is important to understand that a true worshipper who draws near to God's throne in reverent, humble submission to Him in spirit and truth, will also be concerned to worship the Lord in the wider sense of which we spoke in the opening chapter of this book. He or she will not limit worship to a spiritual activity at certain times. Being a worshipper, he or she will want to glorify the Lord in every aspect of his or her life!

It would make no sense for someone to bow in humble and reverent submission to God in a time of worship and then go out and deliberately flaunt His will and deny His claims upon that person's life.

So, although we are going to consider worship in the particular sense of praising God and meeting with Him, we do this aware that His purpose is for us to praise Him with every aspect of our being, in all our activities and in all the circumstances in which we are placed.

3

FOCUS ON THE LORD

It is clear that worship must have an object, the One who we choose to worship. God is by nature a Jealous God and has made clear that our worship is to be of Him alone. We do not worship angelic beings, even though we see in scripture they can radiate so much of God's glory that at times people fall before them as if to worship them. Whenever this happened, the angels always stopped such worship, pointing out that they too were worshippers of the One, true God.

When giving Moses the Ten Commandments, God made clear to His people:

> *You shall not make for yourself an dol in the form of anything in heaven above or on the earth beneath or in the waters below. You shall not bow down to them or worship them; for I, the LORD your God, am a jealous God ... showing love to a thousand generations of those who love me and keep my commandments. (Exodus 20: 4-6)*

Just as we are not to worship angelic or heavenly beings, neither are we to idolise people by putting them in first place of our lives, the place that rightly belongs to the Lord.

When we praise Him and come before Him in reverent love and submission, we are acknowledging that we rightly belong to Him, that He is the Lord of our lives. Although He has made us His sons and daughters we are still to live in reverent fear or awe of Him.

God is our Father, but not in the sense of being a daddy, as you hear some preachers claim. The word "Abba" is indeed the expression of a small child towards his or her loving father. But even Jesus Himself when addressing His Father in prayer, called Him, "Holy Father," and "Righteous Father." He taught us to pray: "Heavenly Father." The sense of intimacy is coupled with the sense of the awesomeness of who God is!

Anyone who has met with the Lord in His glory will immediately identify with this. **The wonder is that this awesome, holy, righteous, heavenly God is our Father.** Because He is our Father, this does not make Him any the less awesome, glorious, holy, righteous and heavenly!

WHEN WE PRAISE HIM AND COME BEFORE HIM IN REVERENT LOVE AND SUBMISSION, WE ARE ACKNOWLEDGING THAT WE RIGHTLY BELONG TO HIM ...

To worship God is to praise Him. Some try to make a false distinction between worship and praise. It is suggested that praise focuses on the majesty and glory of God and is usually expressed in up-beat songs, while worship centers on the holiness of God and is expressed in much quieter songs.

Such a distinction is erroneous scripturally. For example in heaven:

All the angels were standing around the throne and
around the elders and the four living creatures. They fell down
on their faces before the throne and worshipped God,
saying: "Amen! Praise and glory and wisdom and thanks
and honour and power and strength be to our God
for ever and ever. Amen!" (Revelation 7: 12)

When they worshipped God, the heavenly host praised Him! And the words they used are high praise indeed. And yet when they praised Him they fell on their faces in worship before Him.

God is God. You cannot separate His glory from His holiness. **He is "majestic in holiness."** To worship Him in His holiness is to worship Him in His glory! Later we read:

And the twenty-four elders, who were seated on their
thrones before God, fell on their faces and worshipped God,
saying: "We give thanks to you, Lord God Almighty, the One who
is and who was, because you have taken your great power
and have begun to reign." (Revelation 11: 16-17)

There is nothing quiet, dreary or sentimental about this worship. We can see also that it is also false to try and make a distinction between thanksgiving and worship. When the heavenly host worships God, they praise Him and give Him thanks!

However you notice that no matter which word is used "worship", "praise" or "thanksgiving," everything is centered on the One who sits on the throne. The heavenly beings do not focus on themselves, on their feelings at being so close to God. They are not worshipping their experience of God, neither are they singing songs to one another! They are giving glory and honour to Him for who He is and all He has done. They simply want to give Him the praise, the honour and glory that are due to Him!

True worship is focused on the Lord Himself and is directed to Him. We worship what we speak or sing about. To sing of our experience is to worship the experience, a subtle form of idolatry! The experience of God has replaced Him as the focus.

4

PRAISE, PROCLAMATION
AND PRAYER

We have seen that scripture speaks of worshipping God with our bodies, with every aspect of our lives. We are told also to rejoice in the Lord and to sing spiritual songs to one another. The book of Psalms is the "hymn book" of the Old Testament.

The Psalms contain three quite distinct elements:

1. PRAISE

Many psalms are great songs of praise, focused on the Lord Himself. Just one of many examples is found in Psalm 145:

> *I will exalt you, my God the King; I will praise your*
> *name for ever and ever. Every day I will praise you and extol*
> *your name for ever and ever. (Psalm 145: 1-2)*

The Psalmist is speaking directly to the Lord. His focus is on who He is and the praise of which He is worthy. Other Psalms are an encouragement to praise God, Psalm 103, for example:

Praise the Lord, O my soul; all my inmost being,
praise his holy name. Praise the Lord, O my soul, and forget
not all his benefits. (Psalm 103: 1-2)

Here David is speaking, not directly to the Lord, but to himself, to his own soul. He is encouraging himself to take his eyes off his circumstances and to focus them on God, to praise Him and remember all the blessings He has given him. Psalm 149 is addressed to God's people:

Praise the Lord. Sing to the Lord a new song, his praise
in the assembly of the saints. (Psalm 149: 1)

Just as the psalmist encourages himself to give God the praise that is rightly His, so he encourages all the believers, the saints, to do likewise. Is this worship? In the wider sense of the word, that every aspect of our lives is to be lived in worship of God, it is encouraging one another, as Paul advocates.

2. PROCLAMATION

Psalms contain not only songs of praise and encouragement to praise the Lord, they also contain passages of proclamation. They proclaim the truths of who God is and what He has done.

These passages of scripture are wonderful for building faith and greatly encourage us, for they help us to focus on the greatness of God, realising how insignificant our problems and needs are by comparison. These proclamations may be about the Lord:

The LORD is gracious and compassionate, slow to anger
and rich in love. The LORD is good to all; he has compassion
on all he has made. (Psalm 145: 8-9)

Or they may be directed to the Lord personally. A similar scripture reads:

But you, O Lord, are a compassionate and gracious God, slow to
anger, abounding in love and faithfulness. (Psalm 86: 15)

What do we learn from this? That making proclamation about the greatness of God not only encourages our faith, but moves us to praise and worship Him. When we consider how great He is, we are easily moved to worship Him.

3. PRAYER

Although prayers of petition are directed to God, they focus on ourselves, our needs, and the needs of others for whom we pray. There are many passages of prayer in the book of Psalms, and obviously when the Body of Christ comes together it is important to pray as well as worship. Psalm 51 is an obvious example of prayer:

Have mercy on me, O God, according to your unfailing love;
according to your great compassion blot out my transgressions. Wash
away my iniquity and cleanse me from my sin. (Psalm 51: 1-2)

The whole Psalm is a prayer of repentance as David prays for his relationship with God to be restored, having sinned grievously against Him. Many songs that are sung today in services are really prayers set to music. As we can see that there is good scriptural authority for this practice.

So, in the book of Psalms, we see there is a mixture of praise for God, proclamation about Him and prayers to Him. **Proclamation encourages our faith and prayer meets our need, but praise is for the Lord alone.** It is for Him. It is giving to Him what is His due.

PROCLAMATION ENCOURAGES OUR FAITH AND PRAYER MEETS OUR NEED, BUT PRAISE IS FOR THE LORD ALONE.

To worship Him enables us to draw near to Him, meet with Him and hear His voice more readily. Worship brings us to the throne of grace, where we find mercy and grace to help us in our time of need.

If we focus first on the Lord Himself, giving ourselves to Him in worship, we shall be able to receive far more readily than is possible when we pray "from a distance." This is why David knows that it is so important for his close relationship with the Lord to be restored. Then he will be able to worship Him again, not only with his tongue, but also with his life.

Even when David prayed with repentance, he still concentrated on the Lord, on His nature, His mercy and compassion. He is not obsessed with his own feelings of remorse.

We have seen that Paul says there is a place for singing psalms, hymns and spiritual songs *to one another.* Songs of proclamation would fall into this category. We encourage one another by proclaiming to one another truths about our great God and King.

However, we are to make music in our hearts *to the Lord*. Having encouraged one another with songs of proclamation, we now praise and worship the Lord directly by addressing the One on the throne.

We can be very happy when we sing songs of proclamation and that is good. For we are to rejoice in the Lord! But worship is not essentially for our happiness (or even our encouragement!). It is first and foremost for the Lord Himself, to ascribe to Him the praise, honour and glory that is due to His Name. In this way we draw near to the throne and are able to have the wonderful experience of what I shall describe as a "divine embrace" with the Lord of glory!

This is what Jesus has made possible by His sacrifice on the cross, and what the Holy Spirit will enable as we worship in spirit and in truth. Direct access to the throne of grace, to the Holy of holies, or the Most Holy Place, is available to every believer; not just a privileged few.

> *Therefore, brothers, since we have confidence*
> *to enter the Most Holy Place by the blood of Jesus, by a*
> *new and living way opened for us through the curtain, that is,*
> *his body, and since we have a great priest over the house of God,*
> *let us draw near to God with a sincere heart in full*
> *assurance of faith. (Hebrews 10: 19-22)*

It is sad that so many believers have attended numerous services without ever truly drawing near to God in worship, without meeting with Him, having that divine embrace, without having a personal encounter with the Lord. They have sung countless songs, without knowing from experience what it means to worship in spirit and in truth.

Sadly there are many so called worship leaders, who lead the people nowhere instead of leading them to encounter God at the throne of grace. They simply sing songs without any positive direction. One minute they are singing a song of proclamation, then of prayer, then of praise, then of prayer again or of proclamation. It is all a great muddle without any order or direction.

Of course worship does not need to be like this, as we shall see. **It is possible for us to have direct, personal encounter with God whenever we worship in spirit and truth.** We simply need to know how to approach God "with a sincere heart and in full assurance of faith."

REJOICE IN THE LORD

Writing from prison, Paul tells the Philippians:

Rejoice in the Lord always. I will say it again: Rejoice!
(Philippians 4: 4)

Believers need a heart attitude of faith. Instead of being downcast because of their circumstances, they need to focus on the Lord. That, of course, will then encourage them to rejoice, to praise and thank God for His presence and power and provision, no matter what their situation!

Again we see that worship is not to be an activity, but a way of life. A true worshipper will not confine his praise for God to a church meeting; he will rejoice in the Lord always. He will give thanks in all circumstances. His reaction to difficulty will not be to complain, but to pray.

A true worshipper has a worshipping praising heart, no matter where he is, what he is doing or what circumstances challenge him. However, he appreciates the need for specific times when he lays everything else aside, either on his own or with others, to obey the command in scripture to draw near to God, to come right into the Holy of holies, the place where he will find himself on his knees or his face even, before the very throne of God's grace. **As with the host in heaven, so before the glory and majesty of God, he bows in reverent and humble submission, ever mindful of the privilege of being in the Holy of holies.**

It is God's will that we have praising, thankful hearts "in all circumstances." This is one of the things that marks a true worshipper from one who regards worship simply as an activity.

When worship is reduced to the singing of a series of songs, it is possible not to be aware of God's presence. The emphasis is often put on the desires of the people, singing the songs they like to sing, rather than those that glorify the Lord. When the songs are focused on ourselves and our feelings, this is really soulish worship – rather than worship in spirit and truth.

The Holy Spirit has brought the human spirit to life in a born again believer. Jesus makes it clear that the Holy Spirit, who lives in you, "will guide you into all truth." (John 16: 13) He causes you to focus on Jesus, not yourself:

> *He will bring glory to me by taking from what is mine*
> *and making it known to you. (John 16: 14)*

The Holy Spirit is the Spirit of worship, living within the believer. It is He who is to lead our worship at both the personal and corporate level. If the Holy Spirit is going to lead, the worship will become spontaneous, even within a liturgical form of service, for it is not for us to organise the Holy Spirit, but for the Holy Spirit to organise us, in the sense that He will lead us in the way He wants us to go. **That which is soulish is for man's pleasure; that which is truly of the Spirit is for God, to give Him the glory, honour and praise that rightly belongs to Him.**

THAT WHICH IS SOULISH IS FOR MAN'S PLEASURE; THAT WHICH IS TRULY OF THE SPIRIT IS FOR GOD

Many with the responsibility for worship find their security in having a list of songs through which they take the people. This can be without direction as we have seen, and, if we are honest, is often boring for the participants. This is in direct contrast to true spiritual worship which is exciting because it is filled with the presence and power of God. It is always exciting to meet with God, and to encounter Him in a unique way on every occasion. He is never boring and does not become stuck in a boring routine.

Many do not even know that it is possible to encounter God in this way, because they have never experienced such worship. When a congregation has learned to worship truly in spirit and truth they are able to come readily into His presence and can be seen to be meeting with God as soon as they begin to praise Him. His glory invades the meeting. Because they are encountering God personally, many experience being healed by the Lord and have other issues resolved by Him even during the worship - not because they focus on their needs, but simply as a result of the power of His presence. They understand that true worship is for Him not them!

However you cannot give to God without Him giving back to you infinitely more than you have given to Him! This is a spiritual truth, that in giving we receive.

6

NEW DIMENSIONS
OF WORSHIP

In the Book of Revelation we are given an insight into the worship in heaven. All the worship there is obviously in spirit and truth. So this is a model for us, if we really want to worship in the way that Jesus commands.

The move of God we have experienced in worship at Kingdom Faith for several years, began by the Lord saying that He wanted to teach us how to worship truly in the Spirit. I almost felt offended when He said this back in the early 1990s, for we already had a wonderful worship team and our worship was recognised as among the most anointed in our nation.

When I asked the Lord to explain what He meant, He told me that if we stopped doing what we were doing, He would teach us. At that time we did as other charismatic churches did. We had anointed worship leaders, an accomplished group of musicians and sung songs with brief periods of singing in tongues.

In obedience to the Lord we laid all that aside. Having a staff of over fifty and a residential Bible College we have a sizable number of people worshipping together every day, as well as a large congregation that worships together on Sundays. For a period of some weeks we used no worship leader or musicians, neither did we sing songs. And a wonderful process was birthed!

We came to see that worship leaders, musicians and even songs could become props that actually prevented us from worshipping spontaneously in the Spirit, and from developing worshipping hearts. Each one of us learned to depend on the Holy Spirit, the great worship leader, who lives within us. He does not run out of inspiration after five minutes of singing in tongues; it is only our flesh that prevented the Spirit enabling us to worship extensively in tongues. Five minutes, ten, twenty, half an hour. We learned to flow from tongues to English, back to tongues, then English, continuing to alternate for more extensive periods of time.

In this way we were fulfilling Paul's words that we will sing with the spirit but with the mind also (see 1 Corinthians 14: 15). During this time the presence of God among us would become stronger and stronger and people began to have personal encounters with the Lord.

Everyone was aware that we were entering dimensions of worship we had not known before, (and I have been a worshipper for the forty years of my ministry!). Before our worship was much appreciated by people. Now those who came among us were able to encounter God in a new way for there is considerable difference between knowing the Lord's presence and actually meeting with Him.

Suppose the monarch or president was to visit your church for a service. Everyone would be aware of being in his or her presence. But that does not mean that everyone would be given the privilege of shaking hands and having personal encounter with the king, queen or president.

HE TAUGHT US THAT WE HAD NOT TRULY WORSHIPPED HIM UNLESS WE HAD MET WITH HIM; THIS WAS HIS DESIRE AND INTENTION WHENEVER WE WORSHIPPED ...

Christians can be aware of the Lord's presence when they worship, perhaps more strongly at some times rather than others. **Being aware of His presence is not the same as meeting with Him in a way that has an immediate impact on your life. He taught us that we had not truly worshipped Him unless we had met with Him; this was His desire and intention whenever we worshipped,** even though it was not our motive for wanting to glorify Him.

It was at this time that He showed us that the worship of heaven, as described in the Book of Revelation, was to be our model! Now, when we sang songs it was in a totally different way; they flowed out of what the Spirit was doing as He led us.

After the initial period we used musicians again, but they now understood that their job was not to lead, but to accompany what the Holy Spirit was doing in leading His people in worship. One of the singers had the responsibility, not to inspire others to worship or encourage them to do so, but to be sensitive to the Spirit, to know when to allow the flow of worship to continue spontaneously and when to sing a song, or a prophetic song given by the Spirit. **Every believer had come to understand that he or she had to make the decision to worship the Lord with all his**

or her heart, to give God the very best that He deserves. It was not for someone else to have to motivate anyone to praise the Lord.

... GIVE GOD THE VERY BEST THAT HE DESERVES.

Because the Lord showed us this was to be our model, we looked extensively at the worship John the apostle describes in the vision of heaven that was given to Him. At the beginning of this Revelation, John was given a sight of the Lord in glory. As we have seen, he testified: *"When I saw him, I fell at his feet as though dead." (Revelation 1: 17).* We came to see that God wanted to give us such a revelation of His glory that we could do nothing other than fall on our knees or face before Him. This is now a common feature of our extensive times of worship. It is an awesome sight to see hundreds of people on their faces before God meeting with Him.

He wants us to draw near to Himself, right into the Holy of holies; and this is true for every age group. Not only do the youth have their own worship band and know how to enter into the glory of God, but our younger children also praise the Lord in this way. The 7-12 year olds have their own worship band and have their own separate worship time on Sunday mornings. They are often on their faces before God meeting with Him in His holiness. They have become young worshippers, with up to 200 children able to meet with the Lord.

That young children's band now leads worship services and times of ministry all over our nation. It is quite something to see 10-12 year olds packing themselves and their instruments into one of our mini-buses as they go off for a weekend of ministry! Praise the

Lord! As young as they are, they know what it is to fall before God in worship, and can enable others to worship in spirit and truth.

Sometimes in our meetings, all the instrumentalists stop playing because they are on their faces before God on the platform. The worship continues without them, because the people are following the Spirit not the platform! In fact, I don't believe people are even conscious that the musicians are no longer playing; they are too taken up with God to have even noticed.

This is the point: true worship focuses on the Lord, the One who reigns on the throne in glory! True worship enables us to draw near to Him, to meet with Him.

... TRUE WORSHIP FOCUSES ON THE LORD, THE ONE WHO REIGNS ON THE THRONE IN GLORY!

At the beginning of chapter 4, John sees a door standing open in heaven. He hears a voice speaking like a trumpet calling him to -

"Come up here, and I will show you what must take place after this." At once I was in the Spirit, and there before me was a throne in heaven with someone sitting on it. (Revelation 4: 1-2)

As soon as he was "in the Spirit," John saw the throne. This is why God wants us to worship in spirit. He wants us before His throne so we can meet with that "Someone" who is sitting on it! Around the throne there is continual worship. John first describes the four creatures who are closest to the throne:

Day and night they never stop saying: "Holy, holy, holy is the Lord God Almighty, who was, and is, and is to come." (Revelation 4: 8)

You notice how they keep their focus on the Lord, proclaiming in worship who He is. And the response of others around the throne was inevitable:

> *Whenever the living creatures give glory, honour and thanks*
> *to him who sits on the throne and who lives for ever and ever,*
> *the twenty-four elders fall down before him who sits on the*
> *throne, and worship him who lives for ever and ever.*
> *(Revelation 4: 9-10)*

If the glorified ones in heaven fall before God in worship, how much more should we on earth who do not yet have our glorified bodies. Of course this is not some form of ritual; it is the spontaneous response of the heavenly beings to the Presence of His glory! The worship of the creatures moves the elders to worship:

> *They lay their crowns before the throne and say: "You are*
> *worthy, our Lord and God, to receive glory, honour and power,*
> *for you created all things, and by your will they were created,*
> *and have their being." (Revelation 4: 10-11)*

Again you notice how the words the elders speak are directed to the One on the throne.

John's vision continues as he sees the *"Lamb, looking as if it had been slain, standing in the centre of the throne." (Revelation 5: 6)* This is, of course, the risen Christ, who takes the scroll from the hand of God, the scroll that no one was worthy enough to open. Because Jesus alone is worthy to take the scroll and open its seals, the four living creatures and twenty-four elders, *"fell down before the Lamb."* They sing a new song to Him!

You are worthy to take the scroll and to open its seals,
because you were slain, and with your blood you purchased
men for God ... (Revelation 5: 9)

Again we see their words are directed to the Lamb, and they proclaim His worthiness because of what *He* has done. This is true worship. John's vision is then enlarged. He hears "the voice of many angels, numbering thousands upon thousands, and ten thousand times ten thousand. They encircled the throne and the living creatures and the elders. In a loud voice they say:

Worthy is the Lamb, who was slain, to receive power
and wealth and wisdom and strength and honour and glory
and praise! (Revelation 5: 12)

This immense host of angelic beings sing praises. So the worship in heaven is both said and sung. They sing "in a loud voice." It seems these angels give their worship all they have to give. They do not hold back, they worship the Lord with all their strength.

Heaven is going to be very noisy with worship like this taking place continuously. There have been times when I believe heaven has been worshipping with us (or we with heaven). At such times the sound level is difficult for our natural bodies to cope with. (This has not to do with the PA or the playing of instruments, for at such times neither is in use!)

Needless to say, the angels' song is directed to the worthiness of the Lamb. They are not concerned about themselves, or the privilege they have in worshipping the Lord. They are completely taken up with Him.

This is all very well for those in heaven. But does God really expect us to worship in similar fashion on earth? Well, what does John see next?

> *Then I heard every creature in heaven and on earth*
> *and under the earth and on the sea, and all that is in them,*
> *singing: "To him who sits on the throne and to the Lamb be*
> *praise and honour and glory and power, for ever*
> *and ever! (Revelation 5: 13)*

This has to include God's purpose for you! Should you want to interpret this as revelation about the future, let me remind you that we, as the Christian community here on earth, are called by God to live His Kingdom life here on earth! Our lives are to be prophetic, a faithful people living the life now that shall be universally manifested when the Kingdom of God is fully realised, when Jesus comes again in triumph. Our worship on earth is to be at one with the worship in heaven. So the very next verse reads.

> *The four living creatures said, "Amen," and the elders fell*
> *down and worshipped. (Revelation 5: 14)*

When we on earth truly worship in spirit, the creatures nearest the throne say the "Amen" to our worship. And the elders fall down before the Lord and worship Him. John sees heaven and earth worshipping together in unison. And, of course, the worship of God's creation is focused fully on the one seated on the throne and of the Lamb.

By now the evidence is compelling. There is no room in heavenly worship for soulish and sentimental songs. Such songs may appeal to our human emotions (and so are enjoyed by many), but they fall a long way short of true worship.

Nearly all the songs we sing at Kingdom Faith are written by the members of the church here, because there are so few songs in general circulation that carry the anointing of true worship and praise. Others who experience a move of God's Spirit discover the same thing. However, the Holy Spirit is creative, so He will give songs to those who have hearts of true worship.

John later saw the redeemed of the Lord in heaven, *"a great multitude that no one could count, from every nation, tribe, people and language, standing before the throne and in front of the Lamb."* *(Revelation 7: 9).* Again, this must include you, if you are a born again believer! And what is this multitude doing? They are crying out in a loud voice!

Added to the sound of the multitude of angels singing with a loud voice, now we have the multitude of the redeemed shouting their praises! Nothing half-hearted here. No gentle, quiet whispers. God is too great, too mighty! They cried out with a loud voice:

> *Salvation belongs to our God, who sits on the throne,*
> *and to the Lamb. (Revelation 7: 10)*

There is an immediate response from the angels, the elders and the four creatures:

> *They fell down on their faces before the throne*
> *and worshipped God, saying, "Amen! Praise and glory and*
> *wisdom and thanks and honour and power and*

strength be to our God for ever and ever. Amen!"
(Revelation 7: 11-12)

When we the redeemed of the Lord on earth, whose citizenship is in heaven, worship the Lord in spirit and truth, we can evoke a response in heaven. The angelic host joins with us and we with them, but only when we focus on He who is on the throne and on the Lamb. When we truly praise the Lord in this way, the elders fall before the throne and the four creatures nearest to God say "Amen!"

This is a wonderful picture of what worship is supposed to be, and can be, like. It is this worship that the Holy Spirit wants to inspire and enable, *"on earth as it is in heaven."*

WHAT HINDERS US?

If such worship is possible, why is this not the universal experience of the Church?

There are many different styles of true worship. Even we here as one congregation will approach the throne in different ways at different times, depending on how the Spirit leads us. So it is not a matter of saying there is only one right way of worshipping. What I am laying before you here are the biblical principles of true worship, to be applied in the way the Holy Spirit directs.

Religious form is much easier than dependence on the Holy Spirit. There are many denominational forms of worship, where there is little or no expectation, or even opportunity, for people to encounter God in worship as described above. This does not mean that people do not have any experience of God in such formal worship, for clearly they do. But to experience the Lord is not necessarily the same as knowing and meeting with Him in His glory!

There has developed a charismatic/ pentecostal form of worship that is thoroughly predictable, and therefore lacks the spontaneous excitement of true worship in the spirit. Such a form is typified by three or four upbeat songs, followed by two quieter songs, "to build a platform for the Word." The people follow the leader, who often spends as much time talking to the people as to the Lord! When the band stops, the people stop. When the musicians begin, they begin again.

Looking back, I see this is what we used to do until the Lord took hold of our worship and showed us what is really possible. If the people look to men to lead, then they will not learn to follow the Spirit themselves. Every believer has the Spirit of worship within him or her, waiting to be expressed. Of course, the flesh opposes every aspect of the Spirit's authority in our lives, including His desire to make us true worshippers.

THE HOLY SPIRIT URGES THE BELIEVER TO WORSHIP IN SPIRIT AND TRUTH, WHEREAS THE FLESH DOES NOT WANT TO WORSHIP AT ALL.

The Holy Spirit urges the believer to worship in spirit and truth, whereas the flesh does not want to worship at all. If people are walking in the flesh, when they come to a time of worship they will inevitabley depend on others to motivate them and lead them, to cause them to worship. This is not the spontaneous outpouring of love that God wants our worship to be. Because it is spontaneous, it does not mean it will be without order. Whenever the Holy Spirit is in charge, there is always order. If He is leading a congregation, even of thousands, there will be complete harmony and unity, even though what is happening is unscripted and spontaneous. It does not matter whether there is prolonged worship in tongues, repeated affirmations of praise to God, the singing of songs, prophetic songs given by the Spirit, or a compilation of all these things, there will be order as God meets with His people both individually and corporately.

The flesh wants none of this. If there is to be worship, the flesh wants it to be brief. Those who lead in the flesh want to please the people rather than direct them to God by example. Those who follow in the flesh want those on the platform to sing the songs they like in the way that pleases them. They consider that the worship is for their benefit, rather than for the Lord.

I AM NOT GOING TO STOP PRAISING HIM, WHEN I FELL LIKE STOPPING; BUT I AM GOING TO PRESS RIGHT THROUGH WITH GOD UNTIL I AM MEETING PERSONALLY WITH HIM.

The flesh, then, is our greatest enemy. In order to follow Jesus, we have to deny ourselves, to deny the flesh and every soulish attitude. We need to come to every time of worship thinking: **"I am now going to give myself wholeheartedly to the Lord in worship. I am going to give Him my best, for I would not dare to give Him anything less than my best, when He is worthy of so much more than I could ever give Him! I am not going to stop praising Him, when I feel like stopping; but I am going to press right through with God until I am meeting personally with Him."**

At first, you have to make yourself persevere, you want to stop and can become easily distracted. But once you have broken through with God, true worship becomes easier and easier. You can readily come along that way that Jesus has opened up for you to the very throne of God. If this is possible for our 7-12 year olds, it is possible for you!

Of course you need time and opportunity. It is easier to worship in this way corporately; but of course it is possible on your own as well. Unfortunately many pastors withdraw from their responsibility to ensure their people come before the throne when they worship. They hand the leadership of the meeting over to a musician or singer, who has neither the anointing nor the ability to lead the people in such a way that they encounter God. If the one responsible for worship does not meet with God himself, he cannot enable others to do so. The principle is simple. **If those leading focus on God, so will the whole congregation. If they meet with the Lord, so will the people.** The time of worship is not a preliminary to the preaching, but the most important part of the service.

IF THOSE LEADING FOCUS ON GOD, SO WILL THE WHOLE CONGREGATION. IF THEY MEET WITH THE LORD, SO WILL THE PEOPLE.

I am a preacher and I love to preach because this is an anointing God has given me. But I know that my preaching is to come out of my worship for God. If I preach to a body of people that have already met with God in the worship, then the preaching is going to be even more effective!

We have the privilege of having a succession of internationally famous men and women of God to preach at Kingdom Faith. These are much-travelled people who have visited most, if not all, of the spiritual "hot points" in the world. They not only say that they have never encountered the presence of God in such a way as they do in our meetings, but that it is so easy to preach the Word in our church. This is because the people have already met with God and so are open to receive readily from Him.

Lack of time is a great hindrance to true worship. We will give sufficient time, not to the singing of a succession of songs, but to true worship, if we consider this a priority rather than a preliminary. It should never be regarded as only "building a platform for the Word."

I tell preachers: "In heaven you will not be required to preach, but you will have to worship – continually!" I hope some of them will not feel out of place!

We have no time in our church for visiting speakers who want to come into the service after the worship, just before the sermon. If they do not want to worship with us, we have no desire to hear what they want to say! We want to hear messages that come from the hearts of those who want to glorify God.

Worship must always be at the heart of all we do as the Church of the living God, irrespective of our denomination or church affiliation. On Sunday mornings there may have to be a limitation on the amount of time spent in worship, because of sensitivity to the needs of children. In which case congregations need to come together to meet with God at other times when no such restrictions are necessary. At Kingdom Faith, we can give more time to worship at the evening service, during the week and at the conferences we hold. Where there is the will we always find the way! **If we truly want to worship God, we will make the time to do so, and church leaders will provide the appropriate opportunities.**

Once you are used to drawing near to God, it does not take long to do so. But we need to give ourselves time to abide in His presence, to hear His voice and to allow Him to impact our lives in the ways He desires. This is the fruit of worship. Our purpose, first and foremost, is to focus on Him. To give to Him the praise, honour and glory due to His name. To delight ourselves in the Lord.

Although enjoying ourselves is not the objective, those who truly worship in the spirit will certainly enjoy the Lord, and will constantly be both amazed and overjoyed by the way in which He reveals Himself in His mercy, grace and love; in His majesty and glory, in His awesome holiness and power.

It is our flesh and worldliness that oppose the Spirit of worship operating effectively in our lives, and this pleases the enemy, Satan.

8

THE ENEMY'S TACTICS

Satan hates the worship of God. Remember, he was once the archangel Lucifer, whose responsibility was to order the worship in heaven. Then pride arose in his heart. He desired to be as God, the object of worship rather than the one who led worship. Jesus said:

I saw Satan fall like lightning from heaven. (Luke 10: 18)

God will not share His position with any created being in heaven or on earth. Because of his pride, the devil was immediately thrown from heaven along with those angels who followed him in rebellion against God's authority. Because he wants to be the object of worship himself, he opposes worship in spirit and truth. He does not mind lifeless, powerless formal worship because that does not truly glorify the Lord, neither is it a threat to the enemy's influence on people. The enemy will support reasons for not praying or worshipping, suggesting that it will make no difference to do so. Peoples lives and circumstances will stay the same, whether they worship or not, the devil suggests. He implies that people are so useless and ineffective that they might as well not bother to pray or worship. They will inevitably fail to meet with God. Or he wants them to think that they are so unworthy that God would not want

THROUGH HIS SACRIFICE ON THE CROSS, JESUS HAS OPENED UP THE WAY OF GRACE ...

to meet with them, that they would not be welcome at the throne. And he makes it as difficult as possible for them to concentrate! Why are we able to concentrate easily on what we have to do – until we come to a time of prayer or worship?

In other words, being the father of lies and a deceiver, the devil will do anything he can to contradict the truth, to encourage unbelief and suggest that true worship is beyond people. He encourages them to settle for second best, for the known, the predictable, for the safe, for the lifeless even! All this contradicts the commands of God in His Word:

> *Let us then approach the throne of grace with confidence,*
> *so that we may receive mercy and find grace to help us in time*
> *of need. (Hebrews 4: 16)*

There is no mercy for the devil; he is already judged and condemned. So he does not want you to know God's mercy. Because he is condemned, he wants you to feel condemned.

But there is no condemnation for those who are in Christ Jesus. As believers, we stand in the grace of God. His throne for us is the throne of grace, not condemnation. And grace is all God gives of Himself to those who deserve nothing. **Through His sacrifice on the cross, Jesus has opened up the way of grace for those who deserve nothing.**

Pride prevented Satan from worshipping God. And what prevents Christians today from coming before that throne of grace? What prevents them from joining with the heavenly host on their faces before God, being before Him in humble and reverent submission? Is it not their pride?

Does not Satan appeal to the pride that persists in believers' hearts? Does he not cause them to think, "You do not have to worship God that way! You can sit or stand. You can offer a token of praise. You can simply sing, dance and enjoy yourself. You do not have to humble yourself under the mighty hand of God; you do not have to bow like the creatures, the elders, the angelic host."

... WE NEED TO WORSHIP THE LORD WITH TRUE HUMILITY, IN SPIRIT AND TRUTH.

Yes, there will come the time when, clothed in the righteousness of Jesus, we will be able to stand in His heavenly presence. But now we, like Jesus was during His humanity, are made a little lower than the angels, **and like them we need to worship the Lord with true humility, in spirit and truth.**

Certainly we need to resist every lying suggestion of the evil one and his deceiving spirits, that we have no need to worship or are unable to draw near to the throne of grace and meet with God in His glory and power! David says that the saints of God, that is all the born again believers, are to *"tell of the glory of your kingdom and speak of your might, so that all men may know of your mighty acts and the glorious splendour of your kingdom." (Psalm 145: 11-12)*

You can only speak of what you know. **To speak of the glory is God's expectation for all believers.** For you to be able to do this you have to know the glory first-hand. There is no point in thinking you will wait until you are in heaven before you speak of the glory; all those around you will already know the glory for themselves!

God wants you to know His glory first-hand. He wants you to experience that glory, and He desires to impact your life with His glory, so that this glory can be revealed to others through you. What an exciting prospect!

9

PRAISE THE LORD

When the heavenly host worships, the angelic beings, the elders, the four creatures, as well as the redeemed, all praise the Lord. The word "Hallelujah" is literally a command, meaning that all must praise the Lord.

Several different words are used in the Bible for "praise!" Although these convey slightly different shades of meaning, they all basically convey the idea of giving glory and honour to God, of adoring Him, recognising the greatness of who He is and therefore of what He has done.

Because praise places our focus on Him, we come to know Him better the more we praise Him. This does not mean that the more songs we sing the closer we draw to Him. It is possible to sing one song after another without necessarily engaging our hearts with the Lord.

The praise God desires is not a religious performance, but that which is a heart expression of love and devotion on the part of His children. Jesus showed how traditional forms actually hinder the reality of the life that God wants to impart by His Word and through His Spirit. He quoted the prophet Isaiah when He said:

> *Isaiah was right when he prophesied about you hypocrites; as it is written: "These people honour me with their lips, but their hearts are far from me. They worship me in vain; their teachings are but rules taught by men." You have let go of the commands of God and are holding on to the traditions of men. (Mark 7: 6-8)*

Jesus went on to point out to these religious formalists:

> *"You nullify the word of God by your traditions that you have handed down. And you do many things like that." (verse 13).*

These words can have a clear application to formal acts of worship that are lifeless and certainly do not draw people to that place before the throne where they fall on their faces because of the awesome revelation of His glory that is taking place.

Yet even a new congregation can soon become "traditional," adopting a form of worship that becomes rigid and predictable, with little real evidence of the powerful presence of the Holy Spirit, inspiring and enabling the worship. Something has to happen to break out of the mould so that the people can truly encounter God and have their lives impacted by His glory.

Because true worship is essentially a matter of the heart, it cannot be divorced from other aspects of our lives. In the scripture quoted above, Jesus makes it clear that the peoples' worship is in vain because their hearts are far from Him. What does it mean to God to hear the words of praise on the lips of someone who is living in deliberate sin and disobedience?

Those who only praise God when things are going well for them obviously do not have hearts of praise. Jesus goes on to teach that nothing outside a person defiles a person, but only that which comes from within, out of his own heart.

No matter how we feel or what we experience, God is always worthy of our praise, which is why we are to rejoice in the Lord always and give thanks in all circumstances! **The one with a praising heart will meet every situation, even adversity of the hardest kind, with praise.** He knows that God is greater than his situation. In his extremity what he needs to do most of all is to praise God, to exalt him over the adverse circumstances. There is nothing to be gained by complaining about the situation, or being full of self-pity. He needs to give thanks in *all* circumstances, because this is God's will for him.

THE ONE WITH A PRAISING HEART WILL MEET EVERY SITUATION, EVEN ADVERSITY OF THE HARDEST KIND, WITH PRAISE.

So the one with a praising heart will not listen to the deceiving voice of the enemy, when he suggests that it would not be real to praise God if he does not feel like praising Him. The thing that believers most need to do when they do not feel like praising God is to praise Him! This is another instance when we have to deny our fleshly or soulish feelings and responses in difficult situations, and obey the voice of God's Spirit, rather than the lies of the enemy.

A good principle is to keep praising God until you do feel like praising Him! **Usually, the transformation does not take long, for as soon as you begin to focus on Jesus, you will have an**

entirely different perspective on your circumstances. And when you meet with Him, the negative feelings will disappear. This does not mean you should try to escape from the reality of the situation you are in through worship. It is realising that your praise of God releases His presence and power into the circumstances, which He alone has the power to change.

TO STAND BEFORE
THE THRONE OF GRACE
WHEN YOU PRAY, WILL
INCREASE THE
AUTHORITY WITH
WHICH YOU PRAY.

We are told to pray at all times with thanksgiving, to come through the gates of thanksgiving into the courts of praise. When you thank and praise God, it is so much easier to pray and believe that He hears you. John says:

This is the confidence we have in approaching God:
that if we ask anything according to his will, he hears us.
And if we know that he hears us – whatever we ask – we know
that we have what we asked of him. (1 John 5: 14-15)

Approaching God through thanksgiving and praise, encourages our faith and increases our expectation that God will undertake for us. **To stand before the throne of grace when you pray, will increase the authority with which you pray.** You will find yourself doing what Jesus teaches and commanding the mountain of need to be moved. You will pray with the authority of heaven that is yours in Christ.

I tell you the truth, whatever you bind on earth will be
bound in heaven, and whatever you loose on earth will be loosed
in heaven. (Matthew 18: 18)

So there is a close relationship between our praise or worship and prayer. The Lord commands us to praise Him, not because He wants to sit back on His throne and bask in the glory that is His. He knows we *need* to praise Him, to draw near to Him in worship. **He knows our spiritual victory depends on rejoicing in Him always and giving thanks in all circumstances. He knows we will only overcome if our hearts are knit together with His heart in an embrace of adoring worship, while at the same time humbling ourselves under His mighty hand before His awesome glory.**

At Kingdom Faith we have produced a number of CDs and audio tapes that will help you come before God's glorious throne, even when you are on your own. So much "worship" material is available generally, true discernment is needed. It is not going to help your faith to listen to soulish or sentimental songs that will cause you to focus on your feelings rather than on the Lord, who He is and what He has done for you.

HE KNOWS OUR SPIRITUAL VICTORY DEPENDS ON REJOICING IN HIM ALWAYS AND GIVING THANKS IN ALL CIRCUMSTANCES.

Far better to play recordings of true worship that will help to lift you into the heavenly presence of God: worship in which you can participate. This is very different from listening to a performance of songs. They may be appropriate to use at certain times. **But when you need or desire to draw near to God yourself, to meet with Him, hear from Him or receive from Him,** then it is far better to play a recording of true worship with which you can participate. *(Some suggestions of material you can use are given in the Appendix of the book).*

THE HOLY SPIRIT
IN WORSHIP

As you read the Book of Revelation, you will be impressed that around the throne in heaven, God the Father and Jesus, the Lamb, are the object of worship, but not the Holy Spirit. Why is this?

All true worship is in the power of the Holy Spirit, even in heaven! The scriptures tell us that we do not know how we ought to pray; so the Holy Spirit comes to our aid. For this reason we are told to pray at all times in the Spirit.

So also with worship. **We cannot truly worship the Lord in the way that will satisfy Him, without the Holy Spirit enabling us.** Without His help there will be no sense of the Lord's presence, neither will we experience the glory of God impacting our lives. Jesus said that apart from Him we can do nothing. Worship without the inspiration of God's Spirit is worth nothing!

A beautiful performance by a cathedral choir means nothing to God if the worship does not come from the hearts of those singing and unless it is inspired by the Holy Spirit. We may appreciate such beautiful singing for what it is: beautiful singing! But that does not necessarily mean that it glorifies God, or draws us into His glorious presence. We must not confuse soulish enjoyment with the life and anointing of God's Spirit.

On one occasion when preaching during a Sunday cathedral service, the Holy Spirit moved me during the sermon to turn and address the choir. The Lord told the adult choristers that He was not fooled by their outward expressions of worship, when He could see that they were in love with the music more than with Him! At lunch afterwards the bishop said to me: "I am so glad you said that to the choir; they have needed to hear that for years." In love I refrained from asking him why he had not said it to them!

When the Holy Spirit has His rightful place in worship, there will be manifestations or "gifts" of the Spirit. Many of these gifts described by Paul are manifested within the context of worship. The most common gift used in this context is the speaking of tongues, a language given to the believer by the Holy Spirit. Paul says:

I will sing with my spirit, but I will also sing with my mind.
(1 Corinthians 14: 15)

We should not confuse the corporate singing in the spirit, which is a common feature of true worship, with a proclamation in tongues by an individual that requires an interpretation. However, Paul also teaches that one who speaks in a tongue should also pray that he will interpret.

We have learned when flowing with the Holy Spirit in worship, to move from singing or speaking in tongues into our own language, then back into tongues, alternating from one to the other. In this way both your spirit and your mind will remain focused on worship. It is not helpful to be singing in tongues while your mind is distracted, wondering from one topic to another. Your concentration will remain on Jesus, when you learn to flow alternately between tongues and your own language.

THE MORE YOU BECOME ACCUSTOMED TO BEING NEAR TO GOD IN TRUE WORSHIP, THE MORE YOU WILL FIND YOURSELF SINGING PROPHETIC SONGS TO THE LORD SPONTANEOUSLY.

True worship will be prophetic in two ways. God will speak to those worshipping in the Spirit. He may do this corporately, speaking to the assembled gathering through a prophetic song or utterance. However, Paul urges that *everyone* should desire to prophesy. At a service where hundreds or thousands are present it would be impossible for everyone to prophesy one by one. As we flow from tongues to our own language, the worship becomes more and more prophetic.

The Holy Spirit will interpret to you the way in which He is causing you to praise God in your heavenly language. **The more you become accustomed to being near to God in true worship, the more you will find yourself singing prophetic songs to the Lord spontaneously.**

Sometimes these will be so beautiful that you will wish you could write them down. At the end of the worship time it is frustrating to find that you cannot remember these songs. Do not worry, they were not for you but for the Lord. The Holy Spirit was enabling you to sing a new song to Him!

This is a command given several times in the book of Psalms. We are *commanded* to sing new songs to the Lord. These are not in tongues, for in the Old Testament time period that gift had not been given. New songs are inspired by the Holy Spirit. **Every born again believer is able to receive and sing new songs to the Lord.** It is important that those who are responsible for the worship life of congregations encourage everyone to participate in prophetic worship in this way. People must understand that this gift does not have to be left to the same few people giving a public word or song.

EVERY BORN AGAIN BELIEVER IS ABLE TO RECEIVE AND SING NEW SONGS TO THE LORD.

There should not be a rushing into prophetic utterance directed to all present before the people have had the opportunity to meet with God in His glory. A word from the glory of God will have so much more power and will impact those participating in the worship in a much greater way. Remember always, that worship is for the glory of God, not for us to display our gifts. Such gifts as are manifested corporately are to be for the common good, for the benefit of *all* who are present.

There is another sense in which true worship is prophetic. It should be a prophetic anticipation of what will happen when Jesus comes again and His glory will be manifested in all creation. **As His Church on earth we can know, experience and reveal His glory before He Himself comes again in glory.**

When you come together, everyone has a hymn, or
a word of instruction, a revelation, a tongue or an interpretation.
All of these must be for the strengthening of the church.
(1 Corinthians 14: 26)

Only two or three are to give words in tongues with interpretation, or public prophetic utterances. And these are to be weighed. Yet, at the same time, Paul says that everyone has a contribution to make to the worship, for every believer has the Holy Spirit and He can enable the worship of each and every one, as we have indicated.

It is wonderful to hear hundreds or thousands of voices lifted in praise to God, flowing with His Spirit. It is awesome how He will move on a whole congregation, one moment lifting them in high praise into the glory of heaven; then a little later causing an awesome stillness and silence to fall upon the people. At such times no one dare move or make a sound. There is such an awesome sense of God's holiness, and at such times God is speaking clearly and definitely into many hearts and lives.

He has such a great love for His people, that God wants to reveal more and more of Himself to them. He does not simply want to impart information about Himself, He wants us to know Him.

You can only get to know someone by spending time with that person. In worship we can spend time with our heavenly Father, getting to know Him, resting in His love, listening attentively to His voice.

This is what makes worship so wonderful and so exciting for me. It is wonderful to receive fresh revelation of the Lord Himself; not just hear someone talk about Him, or hear what He says in His Word, essential though that is. **Yet I can never get over the wonderful privilege and blessing it is to meet with Him, to be able to touch His glory and to experience His glory touching my life.** And how exciting it is to meet with Him and so be able to receive readily the life He imparts. True worship is never dull or boring. It is not the endless repetition of songs, but meeting with the Lord God Almighty in a living and dynamic way. It is knowing the joy of being at one with Him, through the wonder of His mercy and grace.

And as believers, we have the wonderful hope and expectation that we shall spend eternity in heaven, forever worshipping before the throne of our wonderful God, the Lord of lords and King of kings! See you there!

APPENDIX

The following materials have been produced by Kingdom Faith and are available from:

Kingdom Faith Resources LTD
PO Box 450, Horsham, West Sussex. RH12 4YA
Tel: 01293 854600
Email: resources@kingdomfaith.com

Worship CDs and Tapes
More Fire, Faith '97 *
Yesterday, Today and Forever, Faith 2000 *
I Make All Things New, Faith 2001
Amazing, Youth at Faith 2001
Celebrate the Goodness of the Lord, Faith 2002 *

* *These are double albums and include extended times of worship in the Spirit, enabling you to join in the prophetic flow of the worship.*

Videos
Yesterday, Today and Forever, Faith 2000
Celebrate the Goodness of the Lord, Faith 2002

Teaching Tapes
True Worship

New releases are posted on our website regularly:
www.kingdomfaith.com

There you will find information of the Revival Conferences and Annual Camp where you will be able to experience True Worship for yourself in company with hundreds of others.

Information is also given on the website of the Sunday meetings and conferences that you can view on line.

The True Series will comprise the following titles:

TRUE ANOINTING
TRUE APOSTLES
TRUE AUTHORITY
TRUE CHURCH
TRUE COVENANT
TRUE DELIVERANCE
TRUE DEVOTION
TRUE DISCIPLES
TRUE FAITH
TRUE FREEDOM
TRUE GRACE
TRUE HEALING
TRUE HOLINESS
TRUE JUDGMENT
TRUE KINGDOM
TRUE LIFE
TRUE LORD
TRUE LOVE
TRUE MISSION
TRUE PRAYER
TRUE SALVATION
TRUE WISDOM
TRUE WORSHIP

All these books by Colin Urquhart and a catalogue of other titles and teaching materials can be obtained from:

Kingdom Faith Resources, Roffey Place, Old Crawley Road
Faygate, Horsham, West Sussex RH12 4RU.
Telephone 01293 854 600 email: resources@kingdomfaith.com